THE
BEST OF TIMES

THE

BEST

OF TIMES

Fifty Years of Canadian Sport

TRENT FRAYNE

KEY PORTER BOOKS

CANADIAN CATALOGUING IN PUBLICATION DATA
Frayne, Trent, date.
   The best of times

ISBN 1-55013-102-8

1. Sports—Canada—History—20th century.
I. Title.

GV585.F73 1988   796′.0971   C88-094279-7

88 89 90 91 92   6 5 4 3 2 1

Key Porter Books Limited
70 The Esplanade
Toronto, Ontario
Canada M5E 1R2

*The publisher gratefully acknowledges the
assistance of the Ontario Arts Council.*

Photo research: Dan Diamond/NHL Publishing
Design: Catherine Wilson for
             C.P. Wilson Graphic Communication
Typesetting: Compeer Typographic Services Ltd.
Printed and bound in Canada

Page 1: Rick Hansen circumnavigated the world
in a wheelchair and won hearts everywhere.

Preceding page: In full flight the Golden Jet,
Bobby Hull, was something special: blond hair,
muscles on his muscles, and a pulverizing shot.

Opposite page: Without a misstep or a missplash
in 10 springboard dives in 1984 at L.A., Sylvie
Bernier of Ste. Foy, Quebec, 5-foot-2 and 20,
became the first Canadian diver who ever won
Olympic gold. "The secret," she smiled, "is not
to look at the scoreboard until it's over."

CONTENTS

THE 1940s

THE 1950s

THE 1960s

THE 1970s

THE 1980s

INTRODUCTION

The last fifty years have wrought vast changes upon the games people play. Television, having put every last one of us into box seats, has made each of us an instant expert, perfectly equipped (if inadequately qualified) to second-guess any manager or coach. On the field, too, everything has changed. For instance, where would you find an all-round guy such as Lionel Conacher?

When Lionel Conacher was out there earning his keep in public view, he could do anything—fight, throw, run, hit a baseball, kick a football, cradle a lacrosse ball, or put a fast-skating goal-scorer into the third row of the cheap seats at the end of the rink. In 1950 a poll of sports writers from coast to coast decided that Lionel Conacher was Canada's greatest athlete of the first half of the twentieth century.

The same steely-eyed authors would have a desperate time nowadays picking someone as the greatest all-round performer of the past fifty years. Now everybody specializes. Wayne Gretzky does things with a hockey puck nobody did before, but on the tennis court Wayne the Wizard has two left feet. Ballplayers play ball and that's it. Similarly, since the days of Gerry James, who played football for the Winnipeg Blue Bombers and hockey for the Toronto Maple Leafs, no one has found a way to be a year-round star. What a fuss there was in the summer of 1987 when Bo Jackson, a rookie outfielder for the Kansas City Royals, announced that he'd decided to play football that autumn for the Los Angeles Raiders. The notion that one athlete could perform proficiently in two sports was staggering to U.S. scribes—who stagger easily, anyway.

So here, in the closing decade of the twentieth century, a person would be hard put to set one name above the rest as the best of the past half-century. Gretzky is a giant in hockey; Ben Johnson became the fastest man in the explored galaxy; and surely no one endured a more punishing test or showed more real courage in sports than a solemn, freckle-faced, schoolgirl named Marilyn Bell. Maybe someone will emerge in the century's final decade but, with games growing ever more specialized, it seems unlikely there'll be one dominant athlete rising as clearly above the rest as Conacher did 'way back when.

Conacher's worst game was hockey, but in his time hockey was the only game that offered money for effort. There were ten in his family, five boys and five girls, growing up close to poverty in Toronto in the Depression years. Because hockey meant food on the table, that's where Lionel turned his attention. It wasn't just that he became a star, and later a Stanley Cup-winning coach, but that he also browbeat two younger brothers, Charlie and Roy, into becoming big-league stars as well.

Before that, Lionel had set a Grey Cup scoring record and been an outfielder on the ballclub that won the Little World Series of 1926, a teammate of Hall

Opposite page: **Mighty Mario Lemieux usurped Gretzky's crown in the spring of 1988, taking the scoring championship and then the NHL's prized Hart Trophy.**

of Famers Carl Hubbell and Charlie Gehringer. Lionel was a champion boxer and a champion wrestler and he could kick a football out of sight. One time, after he'd retired and gone into business, he was watching the Toronto Argonauts in a workout. He noticed that the team's punter, Bob Isbister, was experimenting with his kicks. "Maybe I can help, Bob," he said. "Try it this way." In his business suit and street shoes Conacher hoisted a punt eighty-five yards.

Had there been money to be made in lacrosse, Conacher could have worn diamonds. Lacrosse was Canada's national game before it died of a general lack of fan interest. Indeed, it had a role in fathering hockey, the modern-day national insanity. A hundred years ago, hockey's innovators borrowed the goalposts of lacrosse and the idea of faceoffs and terms such as "referee" and "goal."

Before it attracted fandom's ennui, lacrosse drove wild men wilder. An historian, W.G. Beers, was moved once to write of the game's thrills and chills: "Gouty old gentlemen forget their big toes in the excitement of watching a struggle for the ball; the faces of crusty bachelors soften into the old smiles of their youth. Prudes forget their primness, snobs their propriety, old women fearlessly expose themselves to dismantling, young ladies to the demolishment of crinoline and waterfall, dogs will rush frantically over the field and often the ball, and an epidemic of laughter seizes the crowd at the ridiculous incidents and misfortunes of unlucky men." They don't make excitement like that any more.

But if there are no games left that inspire women to expose themselves to dismantling, or drive athletes to the versatile peaks of a Lionel Conacher, it is not to say that the past fifty years have failed to produce marvellous individuals and great moments.

In the 1940s there was Maurice (Rocket) Richard, the first hockey player to score fifty goals in fifty games, a terrible-tempered Mr. Bang who raised hell in high places and was the central figure in a riot in the Montreal Forum and a subsequent rampage through downtown Montreal streets that caused damage in the hundreds of thousands of dollars.

And, also in the forties, there was the round-eyed, doll-like Barbara Ann Scott, the absolute antithesis of the seething Rocket, the winner of an Olympic gold medal in figure-skating at the Winter Olympics at St. Moritz, Switzerland. That decade was memorable, too, for the arrival at second base for the Montreal Royals of Jackie Robinson, the first black player ever permitted by the grotesquely racist lords of baseball to play in their organized leagues.

In the 1950s there was the Mud Bowl, the weirdest Grey Cup game ever played. Across the Atlantic, Marlene Stewart Streit, a freckle-faced youngster from the Niagara peninsula, won the women's British Amateur golf championship, while on Canada's west coast, history was made by a Brit: Roger Bannister became the first person to cover a mile in less than four minutes without benefit of rubber tires.

In the 1960s, Anne Heggtveit tore down a mountainside on slalom skis and won an Olympic gold medal; Northern Dancer ran a mile and a quarter in record time to win the Kentucky Derby; and Gary Cowan won the U.S. amateur golf championship, the first Canadian to sink a winning putt down there since Ross (Sandy) Somerville thirty years earlier. Johnny Longden, a tiny horse rider,

In his time, Lionel Conacher outplayed and outfought everybody. He was a Grey Cup scoring leader, captain of Stanley Cup teams, a boxer, a wrestler, a star ballplayer and he could punt a football out of sight.

brought down his six thousandth winner at age fifty-eight; and George Knudson, playing golf in Arizona, won back-to-back events at Phoenix and Tucson, the first Canadian to manage consecutive wins on the pro tour. George Chuvalo,

George Knudson won eight golf championships on the U.S. tour, including back-to-back victories at Tucson and Phoenix in 1968.

who mastered the art of fighting with his face, went fifteen rounds with the world's champion, a self-effacing, modest, quiet-spoken man named Muhammad Ali.

Imagine, Fergie Jenkins, a fire-balling righthander from southern Ontario, won twenty games for the Chicago Cubs in 1972, the sixth straight year in which he'd won twenty or more in the world's tiniest, windiest ballpark, Chicago's Wrigley Field. Debbie Brill, bright, articulate, lissome, won her first international high-jumping title at the Commonwealth Games in 1970; Bobby Orr arrived from outer space to revolutionize defensive play in 1967 and scored a Stanley Cup-winning goal four seasons later; Ronnie Turcotte won the Triple Crown of racing aboard the magnificent Secretariat; Kathy Kreiner was the first and fastest skier down the mountain at the 1976 Olympics; and in 1977 Jerome Drayton won the Boston Marathon. Meantime, the Crazy Canucks were teaching Europeans a new approach to downhill skiing, somehow without breaking their necks.

Great moments, great names. Alex Baumann setting world records and winning gold medals at the Los Angeles Olympics in 1984. A gold for Sylvie Bernier, too, coming off the three-metre board as gracefully as a falling leaf. Gentlemanly Gaetan Boucher, peerless speedskater, smooth as a Rolls-Royce on the giant oval, winner of two golds at the Sarajevo Olympics.

Was there one great moment in the fifty years which stands above the rest? Chances are, hundreds of thousands of hockey fans would opt for that moment in September of 1972 in Moscow when Paul Henderson's goal with thirty-four seconds left to play won the first summit series between Canada and the U.S.S.R. That moment will live forever because it was the first chill-spiced climax in what has become an international series of grand proportions.

But there are others who contend that, no, the ultimate moment in these confrontations arrived on another September night fifteen years later when Mario Lemieux, who was six years old when Henderson's shot was echoing across the land, beat the Soviets with one minute and twenty-six seconds remaining in an epic three-game series. That was in the autumn of 1987.

In an emotional sense, both factions hold winning hands. Surely no series of hockey games ever clutched the hearts of this country's fans (and thousands of non-fans, too) to the extent of that first one. However, just as surely, there has never been an international series in any sport more exciting, more skilful or more downright beautiful than the 1987 match-up of Canada's finest native-born players and the tireless sons of the Soviet steppes.

How could there be a more compelling demonstration of how the game should be played? The calibre of skill had escalated dramatically in the fifteen years between the two series. Each team had borrowed key elements of the other's style. If the Russians once were sneaky in their aggression, they had now become as openly tough and intimidating as the Canadians of yore. The Canadians, for their part, led by the incomparable Gretzky, had adopted the free-wheeling passing game of the dazzling redshirts, and had injected year-round conditioning into their approach to the winter game.

So this time the sustained speed was breathtaking, the puck control remarkable. A hockey authority, Emile (the Cat) Francis, once said, "Hockey is a slip-

pery game; it's played on ice." In this series, the way the players manoeuvred the puck made it seem that they had it stapled to elastic bands. The passing game on both sides was often uncanny.

The Russians won the first game, in overtime, by 6-5. The Canadians won the second game, in overtime, by 6-5. And then Lemieux came along when the third game was tied at 5-5. The games were played on a Friday, the following Sunday, and the Tuesday after that. Glassy-eyed scribes wrote that Friday's game could not be surpassed. They wrote the same thing about Sunday's. And of the Tuesday game what they wrote was that it could not be surpassed. No way.

Tuesday's began on the lovely, summery evening of September 15, before more than seventeen thousand people in the new Copps Coliseum in Hamilton, twenty-five miles down the road from Toronto. A few million more fans were peering at television screens right across the land. And for them there had scarcely been time for a commercial, the beer may still have been warm in the cooler, when the score was 3-0 for the Soviets. Eight minutes after the opening faceoff.

The visiting forces applied forechecking pressure from the start. Five darting, red-shirted waterbugs with dazzling speed and iron shoulders, they wouldn't let the Canadian defencemen organize counter thrusts in the Canadian end of the ice. They scored after twenty-six seconds of play when a harried defenceman gave the puck away. Seven minutes later they scored again. And less than a minute after that, another. The rout was on.

But, wait.

"We were down 3-0," Rick Tocchet, a hewer of wood who always gave unmercifully of his body along the boards, said later. "We knew we had to get the next goal. We got that one on a power play. Then we got another and we knew we had a chance."

The Canadians increased the pressure on Soviet puck-carriers, finishing off their checks with vigour. Every time a Russian passed the puck he was administered a thumping, punishing hit. The redshirts grew less aggressive in the Canadian end, scrunching up to absorb the thumps. On offence they began unloading the puck a trifle sooner. Their timing was upset.

The Soviets are a marvellous assemblage. Their ability to accelerate is stunning. They cannot be intimidated, but they can be given pause. This happened.

When teams play at this level, the result is spellbinding. Too many people in too many NHL cities never see hockey the way it can be played. H. (for Hidebound) Ballard, the Maple Leafs owner, won't let the Soviets in his building, a policy he says he adopted after Soviet firepower shot down a Korean 747 airliner inside Soviet airspace. But long before that, when he'd refused to book a touring Russian team into his rink to play his Maple Leafs, I asked him why. He grinned wickedly and replied, "Why should I let those bastards show us up?"

Now, though, in the Copps Coliseum, this thrilling game approached its climax with the score tied and another sudden-death overtime looming. In a quick

Opposite page: Who'd believe a pitcher in Chicago's windy bandbox, Wrigley Field, could win 20 games in six straight seasons? Fergie Jenkins did it.

Here's the shot that made history. Taking a pass from Gretzky, Mario Lemieux closes on the Soviet net for the 1987 Canada Cup's winning goal.

exchange, Wayne Gretzky collared the puck in the centre zone and dashed away on characteristic quick, choppy strides along the left boards. Larry Murphy was with him, on his right at mid-ice. They cruised into the Soviet zone and defenceman Igor Steinov moved across to prevent Gretzky from cutting toward the net. Murphy was closely guarded, too.

Suddenly, between Murphy and Gretzky and trailing them by ten feet, there loomed the giant form of cruising Lemieux, a six-foot-four, 200 pound, smooth operator, breathing hard. Gretzky, with patented exquisite timing, slipped a backhand pass into Lemieux's route. Mario, a right-hand shot, gathered the soft pass and saw before him a brief clear opening on the path to the goaltender, Sergei Mylnikov.

None of those time-consuming slapshots for Mario. He flicked his big wrists and ripped the puck over the crouched Mylnikov's left shoulder. You could see the puck hang there briefly against the back of the net before it fell.

The place went nuts.

Opposite page: Ben Johnson, a man of few words, let his feet do the talking in Rome in 1987 when he became officially and irrefutably the fastest man on earth.

Opposite page: Some players have been almost as good, but hardly any dominated the ice as Bobby Orr did during his brief, brilliant hockey career.

Mike Bossy, the Islander sharpshooter, led the New York hockey dynasty to a third Stanley Cup in 1982.

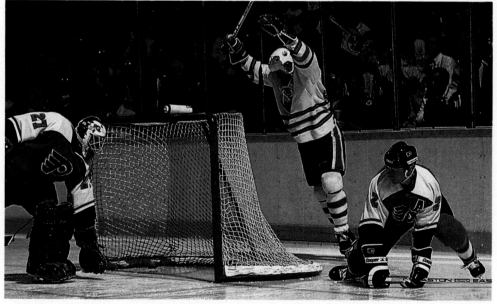

Above: Confrontations between Canada's best and those from the Soviet Union have led to some classic hockey match-ups. The 1984 series (this game was in Montreal) was no exception.

Left: The Great One scores (again) against Philadelphia in the 1987 Cup final.

Ken Dryden stood tall in the Montreal net in the
1970s, backing a great lineup.

Opposite page: Almost everyone was surprised
when veterans Bob Gainey and Larry Robinson
led the Canadiens to another Stanley Cup victory
in 1986.

Following pages: Not since Ethel Catherwood, the
Saskatoon Lily, won the 1928 high jump has
Canada had a woman jumper close to
Vancouver's Debbie Brill.

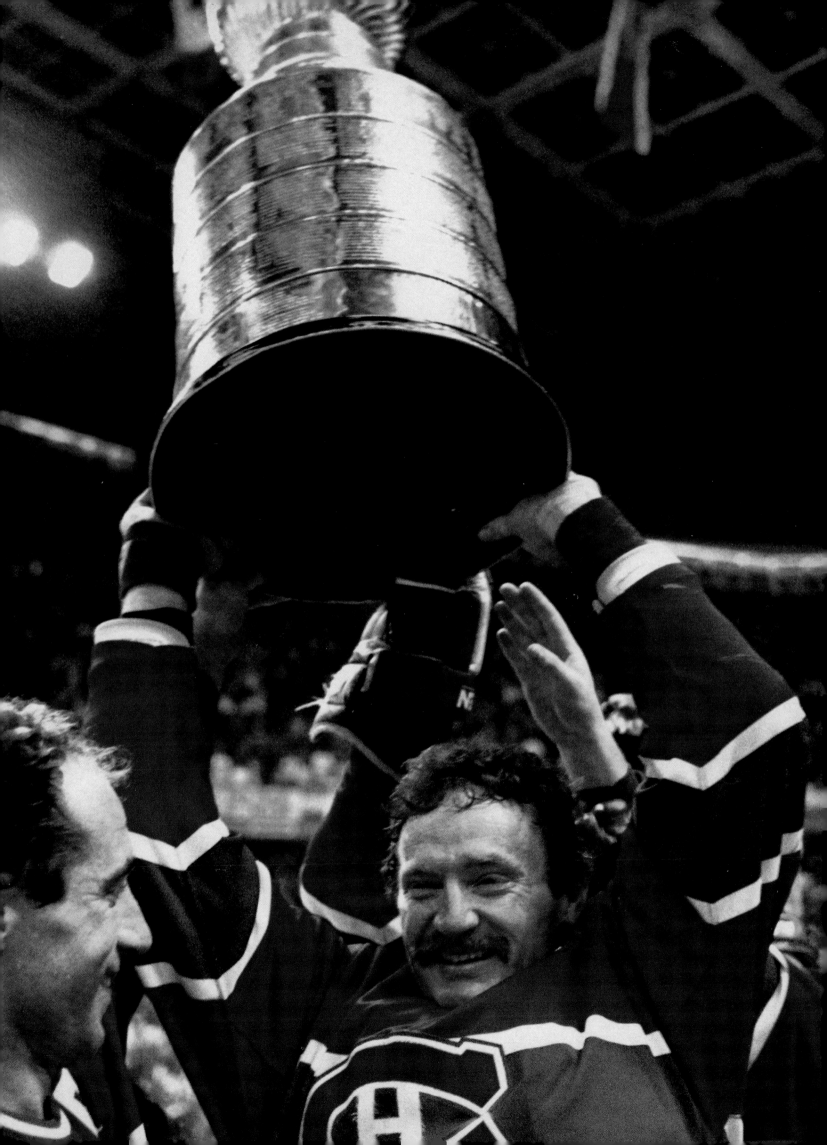

Opposite page: **The intensity that swimmer Alex Baumann brought to competition was almost frightening.**

Tim Raines, a fast man on the bases, has been one of the great Expo players in the 1980s.

Opposite page: In 1987 Edmonton's Henry Williams returned a kick for a touchdown, leading to an Eskimo Grey Cup (not the first).

Toronto Blue Jay George Bell hit 47 home runs on his way to becoming the American League's most valuable player in 1987. Then he flopped.

Brian Orser, the first Canadian World singles
figure-skating champion since Donald McPherson
in 1963, won his second Olympic silver medal at
the Calgary Winter Games in 1988.

The most outstanding performer of all the Crazy
Canucks was Steve Podborski. He took silver at
the Lake Placid Winter Games, and won a slew of
World Cup events.

Elizabeth Manley's happiness was unbridled when she won an Olympic silver medal in Calgary.

THE 1940s

THE VOICE

A great many people remember the final game in Moscow between Canada and Russia in their September series of 1972 as the highlight of Foster Hewitt's broadcasting life, but Hewitt wasn't one of them. For Foster, nothing quite matched the unique comeback by the Toronto Maple Leafs thirty years earlier in the Stanley Cup final. I know this because I asked him once and we wrote a magazine article about it.

These days, not everybody can tell one hockey broadcaster from another, their styles are so similar. When Foster was at it, there were only two voices calling hockey games —Foster's and Danny Gallivan's. The pick here was Foster, but maybe that was because his was the first to go cross-country. Every Saturday night you could catch him on the radio coast-to-coast, working from his gondola in Maple Leaf Gardens.

Those of us who grew up on the prairies listening to him will never forget his weekly greeting. "Hello Canada, and hockey fans in the United States and Newfoundland," he'd say in that measured way of his, his tone verging on excitement. "The score at the end of the first period is . . . ." And then he'd tell us, the millions of us spread across the country, brought together in living rooms and kitchens and bathtubs, and on lonely dark farms and in small snow-packed towns, and in big brightly-lit cities from one ocean to the other, all of us in our mind's eye watching the matchless giants on the ice below.

That was back in the 1940s and earlier, back in the years before television, back when the broadcasts came on at nine o'clock in Toronto, when the first period had usually ended. Nowadays, when I think of those times, I think of myself scraping downy cheeks with a razor, in the bathroom of a boarding house at 55 Donald Street in Winnipeg. It is eight o'clock at night, and I am getting ready for the big Saturday-night date, and Foster is telling me that Sweeney Schriner scored the only goal of the first period.

Sweeney Schriner. Sweeney Schriner lives in Calgary now. We sat in his den during the Winter Olympics there. We talked about that long-ago spring of 1942 when the Maple Leafs lost the first three games of the Stanley Cup final to the Detroit Red Wings and then, with all their fair-weather fans deserting them, back they came with four straight wins, the only time it's happened with the Stanley Cup at stake.

In those times, with no television, Foster had a way in his broadcasts of eliminating the unnecessary. Unlike commentators today, he didn't try to give every detail of a puck's jackrabbit path from one player to another. He'd say, "And here come the Black Hawks, led by Mush March, and"—his voice suddenly rising—"now it's Gottselig cutting in on the net! . . . he's right in front of the goal! . . . and, oh! Broda makes a remarkable save . . . . And now"—calmer again—"it's the Leafs' turn . . . . They're storming back . . . " and so on, his voice riding the roar of the crowd. You always knew where the puck was, and when his voice took on a new urgency you leaned forward in your big easy chair (or paused with your razor), sensing that a goal was coming because you knew that Foster had this gift of seeing goals before they happened, and then you'd hear his cry, "He shoots! He *scores!*"

Opposite page: Where was there ever a voice to match that of Foster Hewitt? He turned Saturday night into Hockey Night in Canada.

35

Above: History is in the making in Toronto's Maple Leaf Gardens on April 18, 1942. After losing three straight games in the Stanley Cup final, the Leafs won four in a row from the Detroit Red Wings.

Opposite page: In the seventh game Sweeney Schriner (11 in white) scored twice on Johnny Mowers.

It became the most famous cry in hockey, but the thing about it is that it just happened; there was nothing dramatic about how it came about. "It just seemed the easiest way to describe it," Foster used to say when people asked him how he'd settled on it. Sometimes, answering, he'd grow a trifle testy, as though he didn't understand the endless fuss. He was a very modest guy.

Foster died at eighty-three in April of 1985. Ten years or so before that, an editor at *Reader's Digest* called me from the magazine's head office in Montreal to ask if I'd ask Foster what Stanley Cup series he remembered as the best he'd seen, and have me write about it under his name in the April issue to coincide with the playoffs. Foster said sure, it was all right with him, and then began deliberating over what series to choose.

"You'd probably pick Canada-Russia if you could," I remarked as he thought about it.

"No," he said, his face brightening. "I think I got more kick out of that Leaf comeback in 1942. And now that I've said that, why not that one?"

And so he reflected back thirty-odd years and, armed with an NHL Guide for reference, he reconstructed the spring of 1942 when the Leafs grew progressively worse as the series moved along. Detroit won the first three games 3-2, 4-2 and 5-2, and everywhere in Toronto people began to sound like pallbearers.

But then the worm turned. The Leafs stopped trying to bump with the rugged Red Wings and, in Sweeney Schriner's phrase, "went back finessing." They won four in a row. They won the seventh game by 3-1. Man named Schriner scored two goals. Man named Hewitt said that was it for him, the one he most liked to remember.

Opposite page: **The Maple Leafs won the Stanley Cup five times in the 1940s. Among the stars were Sweeney Schriner, Billy Taylor, Ernie Dickens and Gaye Stewart.**

Sylvanus Apps led Toronto's Stanley Cup charge
in 1942, then went to war. Five years later he
returned and, presto! the Leafs won again.

Conn Smythe once said goaltender Turk Broda
was so cool that playoff pressure "merely brings
him up to normal." Turk helped win four Cups.

THE ROCKET

Hockey players are an impetuous bunch. They have low boiling points but short memories, and mostly their hearts are awash in the milk of human kindness. They fight at the drop of a stick (or an indelicate word), wrestle maniacally while sprawled on the ice, and then, once pried apart, they forgive and forget and practically embrace on their way to the penalty box.

But not Maurice Richard. Maurice Richard, the bright star of the Montreal Canadiens, the most magnetic player of his time, was also a guy who simmered long over a perceived injustice, brooding far into the night. Then, often as not, he exploded. It was not for nothing that Maurice Richard was called the Rocket.

Once, in the Montreal Forum where the Rocket was merely deified, he was given a misconduct penalty for speaking unkindly to referee Hugh McLean. When a rival player needled him, the Rocket swung at him and drew an additional misconduct penalty from McLean.

He seethed over this through much of the night, tossing in his Pullman berth en route to New York. The next afternoon he spotted McLean walking across the lobby of the Piccadilly Hotel. He leaped from his chair, grabbed McLean by the collar and tried to punch him. McLean was rescued by linesman Jim Primeau, who began throwing punches at Richard, distracting him until cooler heads got the Rocket defused.

When the Rocket glowed in the forties (he was fairly incandescent in the fifties, too) hockey was not dominated by offence, as it became in the expansion, or Wayne Gretzky, era of the 1980s. The game moved at a more deliberate pace. Defence mattered, and goaltenders were not treated as lepers by their teammates. Back then, defencemen not only knew the names of their goaltenders, they were their strong, sometimes violent protectors.

In this milieu, the Rocket became the first man to climb the Everest of fifty goals in fifty games. He did it in 1945, one of his eighteen usually tempestuous seasons in the revered *rouge, blanc et bleu*. He was a black-haired, beetle-browed, glowering presence with a truly uncanny sense of location. He really wasn't much bigger than a rangy middleweight fighter (a shade under five-foot-eleven, and about 175 pounds) but he could be planted with his back to the net, a busy rival draped across his shoulders tugging and pulling and heaving, and somehow when the puck landed near him the Rocket could corral it, tame it, and whistle it toward the goal with a malevolent swipe that would propel it past the goaltender's armour. There never seemed to be a moment when the Rocket didn't know precisely where the net was, even when he was lying flat.

Sometimes the Rocket's goals were so indelibly inscribed upon witnesses' memories that they acquired names of their own—the Toronto goal, the Detroit goal, that Chicago goal. One such was written about in a rare hockey article in *The New Yorker* magazine by Herbert Warren Wind, who wrote that hockey people always referred to it as "the Boston goal." As it happened, I was a minion in the sports department of the old Toronto *Telegram* on the morning that George Dulmage came in, wide-eyed, and described it. Dulmage was the sports editor. He had crawled off the overnight train from Montreal and made his way to the corner of Melinda and Bay streets where the *Tely* stood.

"There never was a goal like this one," he reported of the one that eliminated Boston from the Stanley Cup semifinal. And then, as though describing the final moments of Dr. Frederick Banting's discovery of insulin, he recited the detail of it. In the months and years that followed I was to hear his testimony many times.

Opposite page: Rocket Richard's eyes glowed hot as live coals in the intensity of a game. He's being placated by linesman George Hayes (George hopes).

When Rocket Richard got wound up, he was a hard man to unwind. With his back to the goaltender (Harry Lumley here), he could whirl and hit the net without looking. His sense of direction was uncanny.

Opposite page: Can you believe this: In the 1940s there was often the cry, "Break up the Argos!" Joe Krol was a good reason. He could run, pass and kick.

Black men need not apply was the word in 1946 when Brooklyn's Branch Rickey signed Jackie Robinson and sent him to play ball in Montreal.

The game was tied 1-1 in the third period, and Richard had taken a deep cut over his left eye. He was hurriedly patched up in the Forum infirmary with a bandage across his forehead and around his head. Blood seeped through it, creasing his cheek in a long crooked line to his chin. Late in the game he collared the puck behind his own goal, and Dulmage described reverently how the Rocket peered from below his bandage toward the Boston net, through two hundred feet of smoke and heat and frenzy.

Now he started slowly along the right boards and got past his check, Woody Dumart, with a quick change of pace, and rushed through centre. At the Boston defence Bob Armstrong tried to pin him against the fence, but Richard leaped past him, scraping along the boards. Another defender, Bill Quackenbush, came across and forced him to the corner, driving his shoulder into him. Yet he got free and pushed along the backboards as Quackenbush recovered and came again.

The Rocket, tired and hurt and bleeding, resembled an escaping prisoner making his desperate way along a jail's high wall. His eyes were wild. The stained bandage was pushed to a crazy angle. He lurched from Quackenbush, somehow worked his way past the side of the net, and as the goaltender, Sugar Jim Henry, dived to smother the puck on his stick, the Rocket pulled it clear, took a falling stride to the front of the goal and lifted the puck over Henry into the net. Then he collapsed.

BARBARA ANN

According to the prime minister of Canada, the ingredients that Barbara Ann Scott brought to her fellow Canadians in the darkest days of the Cold War following World War Two were "the courage and strength to help us through the gloom."

William Lyon Mackenzie King was as delighted as any skating fan by the triumphs on frozen foreign ponds of Ottawa's sweet-tempered, round-eyed, perpetually ladylike Barbara Ann in the late 1940s, "when you have shone forth like a bright star in a troubled world."

When she won her Olympic gold at St. Moritz, Switzerland, in 1948 Barbara Ann was acclaimed as the nearest thing to Norway's fabled Sonja Henie, who'd won in 1928, 1932 and 1936. Four decades later, she was still so admired and well-remembered that she was the person picked to carry the Olympic torch first from St. John's, Newfoundland, in its cross-country journey to Calgary for the Winter Games.

Also, in 1988, a full forty years after her victory on an uncovered rink in St. Moritz, she was invited to head tables at celebrity dinners in Toronto and Hamilton and Ottawa, a tiny, slender, stylishly-attired woman in her late fifties, her white-blonde hair pulled severely back in a bun from her smiling features. And those eyes, those eyes; they were still the round blue shining buttons they'd been in ten thousand photos in the late 1940s.

Barbara Ann Scott was easily the best skater of her time, twice world champion, twice European champion, twice North American champion, and adored by crowds across Europe when she toured Stockholm, Copenhagen, Antwerp, Paris, London, Oslo, Bern and Lausanne, the Olympic capital in Switzerland, following her gold-medal achievement at St. Moritz.

In Barbara Ann's time there was great emphasis on figures in figure skating, a full sixty per cent of a skater's performance. A few years later the percentage was dropped to thirty, and in May 1988 the International Skating Union (ISU) voted to abolish figures altogether for senior events in international competition, including the Olympics and the world championships. Nowadays, spectators in packed arenas and in front of television screens across a quarter of the globe are bedazzled by the free-skating acrobatics of, say, the East German peachcake, Katarina Witt, and by the pairs wizardry of the brilliant Brits, Jayne Torvill and Christopher Dean.

The figures were enormously demanding. "In my day," Barbara Ann said during the Calgary Olympics, "you often didn't know until the night before which six of the seventy figures you were going to have to do. You really had to know them all."

A contemporary of hers, former American and Olympic champion Dick Button, turned up in Calgary as a television commentator, and remembered her as a brilliant skater in her free-skating programs as well as in the school figures.

"There was nobody to challenge her who was better in one particular area, either compulsory figures or free skating," Button recalled. "Everything was right, everything was perfect. She was delicate, precise, exact, meticulous."

Going into the Olympics, she was nineteen. By then she was acclaimed as Canada's darling, in part because of the boorish behaviour of Avery Brundage, the longtime

Opposite page: **"She was delicate, precise, exact, meticulous," a critic said once of Barbara Ann Scott. She was Canada's ambassador, too, a true champion.**

Olympic czar as president of the self-appointed, self-perpetuating kangaroo court that calls itself the International Olympic Committee (and some call the Waxworks). Brundage was what the American columnist Red Smith termed, "a symbol of the IOC, a rich and righteous anachronism, a vestigial remnant of an economy that supported a leisure class that could compete in athletics for fun alone."

Anyway, in 1947 after Barbara Ann had won the European championship in Davos, Switzerland, and the world championship in Stockholm, she returned to wild acclaim in Canada. On the day she reached Ottawa, school kids were given a half-holiday, police and firemen provided a guard of honour, the streets were thronged, bands played and happy people cheered. Mayor Stanley Lewis gave the returned goddess the keys to a yellow Buick convertible with the licence plate 47 U 1.

Enter unsavoury Avery. He ruled that the gift contravened the rules of amateurism. If she didn't forfeit the car, the old grump grumped, she couldn't skate at the Olympics next year in St. Moritz. If she accepted other proffered gifts—jewellery, a movie contract—the same fate awaited her.

Outrage ruled the land. In Brandon, Manitoba, Avery was burned in effigy. Columnists fumed. James Alexander Coleman wrote an open letter to Barbara Ann in *The Globe and Mail*: "We read in the public prints where some acorn named Avery Umbrage, who lives down in the Excited States, is trying to have you expelled from amateur ranks . . . ." And so forth.

Into this boiling cauldron stepped the young woman herself to still the rising tumult. "It would be selfish of me to keep the car and lose a chance to bring honour to Canada in the Olympics."

And so she did. And won an Olympic gold medal, too. And then she got her car back.

Forty years after winning her Olympic gold, Barbara Ann Scott warmed interviewers and banquet audiences with her charm and her enthusiasm.

Johnny Longden was the most successful jockey ever to call Canada his home. He grew up in Taber, Alberta, and won the U.S. Triple Crown on Count Fleet in 1943 (right). Longden won 6,032 races in a 40-year career, the first rider anywhere who won 6,000. Later (below) he became a trainer.

Following page: Gérard Côté, a policeman from St. Hyacinthe, Quebec, practically owned the Boston Marathon in the early 1940s. He won the grind four times.

THE 1950s

Only the faces change over the years in Stanley
Cup celebrations. Here, Detroit's Terry Sawchuk
kneels with the battered mug in 1954.

Before television, hockey broadcasts featured the Hot Stove League during intermissions. It was live radio on Saturday nights and the panelists became famous across Canada. This panel spotlighted Bobby Hewitson, Jack Dennett, Baldy Cotton, Wes McKnight and Syl Apps.

Opposite page: Goaltenders didn't wear masks when Terry Sawchuk was a star in the Detroit net. He absorbed 400 facial stitches.

Bill Barilko, a blond, curly-haired defenceman, gave the Toronto Maple Leafs their sixth Stanley Cup in ten seasons with this shot in 1951. Goaler Gerry McNeil is down and Captain Henri Richard is out. Later Barilko flew on a hunting trip and died in a plane crash.

MARILYN

For most people on this dullish September afternoon in Toronto, it was just another day at the office, another Thursday to be endured before the welcome weekend. Soon they'd be departing from their downtown office boxes, heading home.

And then, a little past four, quiet word began to spread that Marilyn was still in the water. Two radio stations had boats out on the lake and their reporters were saying excitedly that Marilyn was still in the water.

Who was still in the water?

Marilyn, Marilyn Bell. Not Florence Chadwick, the imported star who came for the money, but Marilyn Bell, the little Toronto school kid. She was still in there after seventeen hours. Hey, how about that? Let's go have a look.

In this fashion offices began to empty and traffic jams began to swell on the streets leading to the big annual exhibition on the lakefront. Car radios were turned on and people were calling to one another that this Toronto school kid would soon be landing on the lakefront down at the Ex.

This was not how it had been planned. For this September day in 1954, the tallest foreheads at the Canadian National Exhibition had brought in Florence Chadwick, a powerful thirty-four-year-old American considered to be the world's best woman swimmer, as a crowd-drawing attraction. She'd been advanced $2,500 and would pick up another $7,500 if she swam across Lake Ontario from Youngstown, New York, to the CNE waterfront. The distance was about twenty-five miles in a straight line, but winds were tricky and the crossing could be ten or twelve miles longer for a swimmer.

So the start time was left to Chadwick's discretion. Because the weather was windy and cool she delayed her departure for two days while reporters from Toronto's two afternoon newspapers, the *Telegram* and the *Star*, scrambled and connived for stories, building up the event.

Meantime, two other swimmers, Winnie Roach Leuszler, who had swum the English Channel three years before, and this young schoolgirl, sixteen-year-old Marilyn Bell, arrived at Youngstown with no promise of reward. Leuszler hoped somebody might pass a hat for her if she made it. Young Bell, who eight weeks earlier had been the first woman to complete a twenty-five mile swim off Atlantic City, was there apparently because her trainer, Gus Ryder, was trying to promote his swimming club.

Suddenly, at ten-thirty on the calm night of September 8, Chadwick took off in the dark for the faraway shore. Leuszler and Bell had to hurry into their swimsuits and get their bodies greased to protect them against the lake's chill. They dived in a half-hour after Chadwick's departure.

Because of Marilyn's youth and the comparative obscurity of marathon swimming, nobody outside of swimming's small circle knew much about her. In truth, she had been an accomplished performer in the water for half a dozen years. Her father had taught her to swim when she was four, encouraged her to pursue the sport as she was

Opposite page: The ordeal of Marilyn Bell began in the flat black waters of Lake Ontario, 53 minutes before midnight on September 8, 1954.

growing, and by the time she was thirteen she was giving swimming lessons to crippled children. At fourteen, she was a professional instructor.

But it was the highly-publicized Chadwick who received the attention. Not until she and Leuszler were beaten by the cold, choppy water did Marilyn's name burst across the city and, with the CBC joining in, the entire country. Chadwick was out of the water, sick and retching, six hours after she began, and Leuszler was compelled to quit in an agony of stomach cramps several hours after that.

Leaving Marilyn. Amazingly tiny for such an ordeal, only five-foot-one and 117 pounds, she possessed the heart and tenacity of an alley cat. Because of Chadwick's unexpected plunge into the lake in the dark, the schoolgirl had gone all day without sleep, had swum all night and now, in the late afternoon, she was still seven miles from her goal, and ready to quit for the fourth time. She was barely conscious. She would swim a couple of strokes, then tread water. She was whimpering and crying. From time to time her trainer scrawled messages on a blackboard. "Flo Is Out," and "Don't Let the Crippled Kids Down." Marilyn was haggard. Pain probed her arms and legs. Her stomach throbbed. A lamprey sucked at her thigh. Shuddering, she knocked it away. More eels attached themselves to her. She pushed them off.

Somehow, from some channel of reflex or resolve, came the message for a fourth time to keep going. She began her stroke and, incredibly, never faltered again. She moved achingly ahead, stroke by stroke, breath by breath, until she had crawled through the black waters to the concrete wall that ended her quest. She had covered more than thirty miles, had been in the water for more than twenty-one hours. Yet even then, her face white with strain and sleeplessness, her mind numb, she struggled against her trainer and a reporter who lifted her into the boat. She still resisted help, still struggled to go on and on and on.

Above: As a muscular towhead of 18, Cliff Lumsdon won a 15-mile marathon swim in Lake Ontario, then repeated four times in the next five years. He won $30,000 in a 32-mile ordeal and won Atlantic City swims, too.

Left: After 21 hours of numbing cold, the barely conscious Bell touched the breakwater at Toronto's waterfront, ending her ordeal.

Legendary rowing coach Frank Read (above) turned the University of British Columbia into Canada's rowing capital. Of his four-without-coxswain gold medal winners in 1956, none had rowed a year earlier. Read's method was once described as ''pitiless and painful.''

Top: Bob Hayward drove the fastest hydroplanes in the world in the late 1950s, the two Miss Supertests. He died in a spill.

Above: Maritime slugger Yvon Durelle knocked down world light-heavyweight champion Archie Moore four times but, still, Archie got up and won.

Right: In the 1950s when the U.S. golf tour began to burgeon, one of the best Canadian tourists was Toronto's Al Balding, who had been building tires at Toronto's Goodyear company.

Marlene Stewart Streit shot birdies everywhere. She won the British Amateur, the U.S. Open and took uncounted titles at home in Canada.

Stan Leonard, long-hitting pro at Vancouver's Marine Drive club, won three times on the U.S. men's pro tour.

Opposite page: In perfect harmony, Frances Dafoe and Norris Bowden won world pairs titles in 1954 and 1955 and an Olympic silver in 1956.

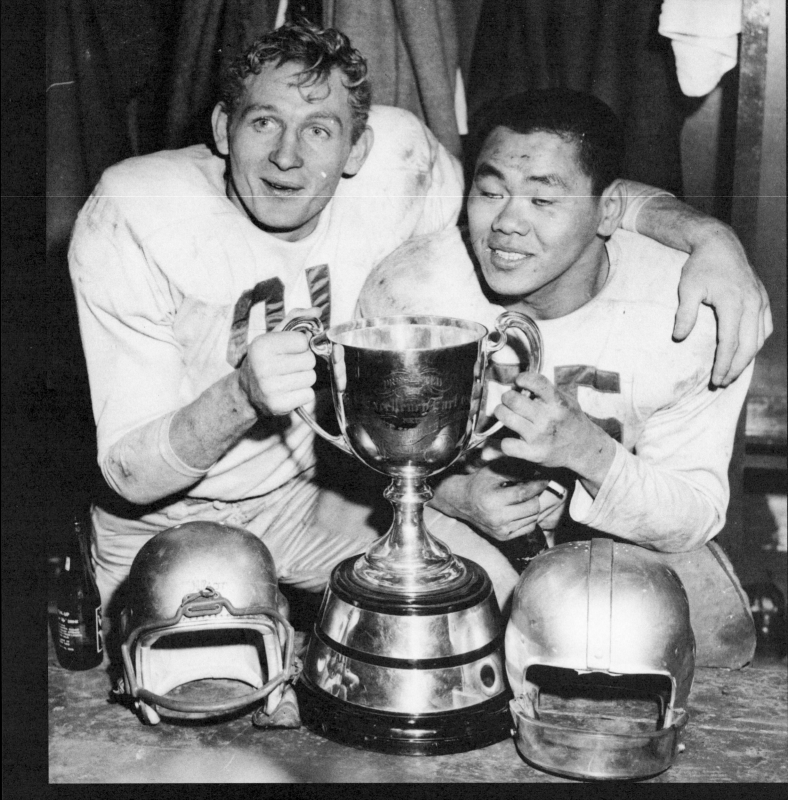

JACKIE PARKER

It is no news to sports historians that the Grey Cup game gained its first national attention in 1935 when the Winnipeg Blue Bombers, ignited by the darting little halfback Fritz Hanson, achieved the west's first victory over the eastern champions.

Similarly, sociologists are aware that public lunacy, as it relates to football, was introduced in 1948 by a trainload of Calgary zealots of both sexes. They paraded on horseback and buckboards on Toronto's Bay Street disguised as cowpokes wearing five-gallon hats and ten-gallon hangovers, and flipped flapjacks to dumbfounded throngs on the sidewalks.

However, real fans recognize that the game itself wasn't really implanted in the national psyche until nearly twenty years after the Hanson heroics. It was then, beginning in 1954, that Jackie Parker and his Edmonton Eskimo teammates won the big game three years in a row and forever put the boots to the east's arrogant dominance.

Parker's part cannot be exaggerated. He ran ninety yards with a recovered fumble in the waning moments of the 1954 game, contriving a 26-25 victory; he was voted the 1955 game's outstanding player; and in 1956 his nineteen points on three touchdowns and a kick to the deadline set a Grey Cup scoring record.

Parker was abetted by a revolutionary offensive system that discombobulated eastern rivals. This was the split-T, an offence favoured by the powerhouse teams of Bud Wilkinson at the University of Oklahoma. Because of Oklahoma's success, the Eskimo manager Al Anderson decided on a whim to call Wilkinson and ask him to recommend a split-T coach for Edmonton.

The coach turned out to be Darryl Royal, an assistant at Mississippi State later canonized for his enduring success coaching the University of Texas Longhorns. In Edmonton in that year of 1953 Royal and the split-T were instant successes with a 12-4 won-loss record, though Winnipeg shaded the Eskimos in the western final. Then Royal left to become head coach at Mississippi State.

That move sent Al Anderson back to Bud Wilkinson for another recommendation. Wilkinson, delighted by the split-T's reception up north, permitted his own top assistant, Frank (Pop) Ivy, to succeed Royal, and of course Pop was even more successful with the Eskimos than Royal had been.

The split-T differed from conventional offences in that the linemen didn't crouch shoulder-to-shoulder but spread, or split, anywhere from two to four feet apart. That alignment, common in later decades, spread the defence, opening holes through which halfbacks could dive and fullbacks charge and the quarterback occasionally sneak. The advantage of the system was that linemen needed only to sustain holes, not flatten somebody to open them.

For instance, in the 1954 game a comparative shrimp like 215-pound Dale Meinert had no trouble with Montreal's 260-pound Tex Coulter; he didn't have to knock Tex down, he only needed to ward him off long enough for somebody to squirt past with the ball.

Although the split-T derived its name from the split line, the key operator was the quarterback. Once he took the ball from the centre his job was to drift up or down the line. He could hand off the ball to backs charging past or flip it to a back running

The Edmonton Eskimos began a reign of terror in 1954, winning three straight Grey Cups featuring Jackie Parker and pile-driving Normie Kwong.

wide or burst through the line with it himself. Or he could pass it, and of course on every play he went through the motions of doing all four of those things, faking baffled defenders out of their athletic supporters.

In the 1954 game the formation was so new to the perplexed Alouettes that once when the Edmonton halfback Normie Kwong apparently took a handoff from the quarterback Bernie Faloney he was nailed by Coulter and an official standing over them was about to blow his whistle to terminate the play.

"Don't blow it! Don't blow it!" cried Kwong. "I haven't got the ball!" Across the field Faloney was flipping it to Parker running wide.

Parker played halfback that year (he moved to quarterback in 1955 when Faloney went into the U.S. army). He was a mighty peculiar looking football player: pigeon-toed, linguine-legged, with a curious walking motion, long arms and ham hands swinging as though he were steering a canoe. But he could do everything—run, throw, kick. He was a flaxen-haired, drawling native of Tennessee, a graduate of Mississippi State, a split-T school at which he illustrated his dedication to football in a manner never demonstrated before or since.

He was unable to get a football scholarship at a Southeastern Conference college because he was married, so, with an opportunity to get into Mississippi State, he and his wife Peggy Jo decided to get a divorce. They'd been married when Parker was sixteen. A year later, Jack became the leading scorer in U.S. college ball and he and Peggy Joe were married all over again. (Later, they were divorced again, too, after producing a son and two daughters.)

Actually, by the time he was twenty-three and driving defences dizzy on the Canadian steppes, the amiable Parker had had one wife, two marriages, a divorce and six years of matrimony. People who opposed him on playing fields felt that he was unique there, too.

Some say Hal Patterson was the best all-round player in CFL history. He was an Alouette star in the mid-fifties, then went to Hamilton.

Opposite page, top: Only Sam Etcheverry, the Montreal quarterback (92), had a chance to catch Parker in Jackie's famous field-length dash. But Sam missed.

Opposite page, bottom left: Montreal's Sam Etcheverry was called The Rifle, an all-time great. In the 1955 Grey Cup game, Sam passed for a record 508 yards. Still, the Als lost.

Opposite page, bottom right: Gotcha! Royal Copeland caught Joe Krol's passes in three Grey Cup years for the Argonauts: 1945, 1946 and 1947. Cope was a Stampeder, too.

Following pages: Even mud wrestlers would have shunned the quagmire of Varsity Stadium for the 1950 Grey Cup game. The mud-caked Toronto Argonauts beat the Blue Bombers of Winnipeg on a mild November afternoon after a snowfall. Coach Frank Clair sits behind the trophy.

History in Vancouver's Empire Stadium in 1954: Roger Bannister shaded John Landy and broke the four-minute mile for the first time.

THE 1960s

Preceding pages: Born to ski: Anne Heggtveit's mother had her on skis at age two in Ottawa's Rockcliffe Park. At 17, although not fully recovered from a broken leg, she was twenty-second in slalom racing at the Cortina Olympics. At 21, she zipped over Squaw Valley's slalom course for a gold medal.

Above and right: Nancy Greene left few skiing worlds unconquered. Born in Ottawa and raised in Rossland, B.C. she fled down mountains in three Winter Olympics, won gold in 1968, was World Cup champion twice, was Canada's Athlete of the Year, and became a Member of the Order of Canada.

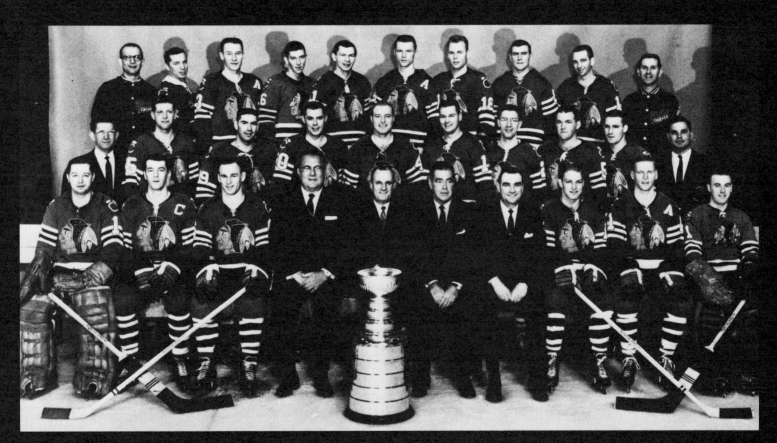

Are the Chicago Black Hawks and the Stanley Cup a contradiction in terms? No, the Hawks won it in 1961 with Glenn Hall (front left), Stan Mikita (back, fifth from left) and Bobby Hull (front, third from right). The coach was Rudy Pilous (front, fourth from right).

Top: Gordie Howe spoke softly and carried a big stick. This goal on Montreal's Gump Worsley was number 544 and broke Rocket Richard's mark.

Above: Whooping it up are 1964's Stanley Cup-winning Toronto Maple Leafs. Captain George Armstrong bows his head by the trophy. Frank Mahovlich, upper left, salutes his dentist.

Opposite page: Punch Imlach put so many veterans into uniform in the 1960s that comedian Johnny Wayne remarked: ''When most teams win the Stanley Cup they drink champagne and go out on the town. The Leafs drink warm milk and go to bed.'' They won four Cups.

In 1962 in Prague, Canadian skaters produced their finest week. Don Jackson (opposite page) won the world men's title (he executed the first triple Lutz in international competition); Maria and Otto Jelinek (top) won the pairs; Wendy Griner (right) took a silver medal; and Virginia Thompson and Bill McLachlan (far right) a bronze.

Above: 1964's bobsled gold medalists were dubbed The Intellectuals. Vic Emery graduated from Harvard, Doug Anakin from Queen's, Peter Kirby from McGill and John Emery was a plastic surgeon in Montreal.

Right: Regina's Ernie Richardson skipped his famous rink to five provincial, four Canadian and four world curling titles, an unmatched record. In the first three, Ernie teamed with brother Sam and cousins Arnold and Wes Richardson. For the fourth, Mel Perry replaced Wes.

Smiles of gold belong to Barbara Wagner and Bob Paul, Toronto skaters who won the pairs title at Squaw Valley's Winter Olympics in 1960.

THE DANCER

In this tableau that has been vivid for nearly a quarter of a century, the little horse, Northern Dancer, is in front in the stretch at Churchill Downs. It is the Kentucky Derby of 1964, of course, the one and only time a Canadian-bred horse won the most ballyhooed gallop of thoroughbreds on earth.

He was always called the little horse, Northern Dancer was. In truth, he wasn't all that little. What he was, he was *stocky* little. He was little the way a hydrant is little. He was built like a middleweight fighter.

In this tableau he is running the way he always ran, with a sort of earnestness, if you can imagine that in a horse, with his neck thrust straight out, his muscled chest heaving, his hooves performing that stiff-legged *kra-thump, kra-thump, kra-thump* rhythm of thoroughbreds at full throttle, and the dude on his back, the snarly Bill Hartack in the turquoise-and-gold shirt of Windfields Farm, is pumping his whip into the horse's rear left upper thigh with every stride as he comes down along the rail.

They are in the stretch, a couple of hundred yards from the wire, and closing on them, inching ever closer along the Dancer's right flank, is this California-bred race favourite, Hill Rise, and on Hill Rise's back is a rider who has been around the block and back a few times himself, Bill Shoemaker. Everything else in this race is up the track.

Now, at this time Northern Dancer is three years old, with no hint that twenty years down the road he will have become the most astonishingly productive stallion of his time. Here, running, he is just a very promising three-year-old, a late three, at that, who didn't see the light of day until late May in 1961. He was late because his owner, Edward Plunkett Taylor, and E.P.'s right arm in racing, Joe Thomas, didn't decide until very, *very* late in the mating season of 1960 to set up a union between the parents, the sire Nearctic and the dam Natalma. This was because Natalma was an excellent race mare who had been injured, and rather than wait for her to mend, the Windfields brain trust decided to breed her.

And what arrived on May 27, 1961, was this foal with a white blaze on his forehead that extended down inside his left nostril, and three white feet. Back then, Taylor held an annual pre-priced sale of his yearlings; that is, on the year's crop of fifty or sixty unraced colts and fillies at Windfields, E.P. would set a price on each, and anybody who wanted to buy one could do so at that fixed price. The horses left over when the buyers went home were kept and raced in the Windfields silks.

The price on Northern Dancer was $25,000. That seemed fair enough: although he was well bred, he was smallish by most standards, short and blocky at fifteen hands. (That's a little over five feet, measured at the withers, his front shoulder blades. Most top runners, such as Hill Rise, the Dancer's archrival in the Kentucky Derby, go sixteen hands—about four inches taller.) But he went unclaimed at the pre-priced sale, perhaps because of his size.

What nobody guessed was that this colt had "prepotent" qualities, something that David Macfarlane went into in his prize-winning article on breeding in *Saturday Night* magazine in September of 1987: "A prepotent stallion passes on his own strengths as

Opposite page: Blue bloods in the blue grass laughed at the idea of a Canadian-bred horse winning the overly-romanticized Kentucky Derby. But in 1964 E.P. Taylor's Northern Dancer, Bill Hartack riding, beat Hill Rise in two minutes flat, record time for the Derby's mile and a quarter.

In the winner's circle after the Derby victory, the Dancer wears garlands and accepts due praise.

Opposite page: Edward Plunkett Taylor made Canadian racing world class in the 1950s, and in 1964 bred Northern Dancer, who became the world's leading sire.

well as the strengths of his ancestry. Northern Dancer's bloodlines were impeccable—both parents were descendants of some of the most distinguished thoroughbreds in history."

Passing on this prepotency (if that's what it was) the Dancer sired the most expensive and some of the most successful race horses ever. His second crop included the English Triple Crown winner, Nijinsky II, in 1970. Seven years later his son, The Minstrel, won the Epsom Derby and became British horse of the year; and seven years after that, two of his sons, Secreto and El Gran Senor, finished one, two in the Epsom Derby. Expensive? In 1983 at the Keeneland yearling sales in Kentucky a son of his sold for a record $10.2 million. Two years later, a grandson brought $13.1 million.

How did this happen? Mostly because in the mid-1970s thoroughbreds became an international currency, like paintings. Multimillionaires got caught up in the search for dominant bloodlines. Bidding at auction for the offspring of successful sires, such as Northern Dancer, hit dizzying altitudes.

Even so, it's the ancient tableau that persists. Hill Rise comes on. Shoemaker has him in full drive. Inch by inch he moves up. He is at the Dancer's flank, his girth, his shoulder, his neck. But then the advance suddenly stops. The Dancer is fighting him off. There is that earnestness, you know? His neck is out. All you can wonder is: Can the little Canuck hang on?

And now he is under the wire, and of course he hung on. Was there ever a doubt?

Opposite page, top: Mayor Jean Drapeau (right) put big-league baseball into Montreal's quaint and charming Jarry Park in 1969. Superfan Mike Pearson threw out the first ball. Oh yes, Mr. Pearson was also the prime minister.

Opposite page, bottom: Where to find a story stranger than that of university students Roger Jackson and George Hungerford? Teamed only two weeks before the Tokyo Summer Olympic Games, they won the pairs-without-coxswain event in 1964.

On the last day of the 1968 Summer Olympics in Mexico Canadian equestrians Jim Day, Tom Gayford and Jim Elder collected gold medals from Prince Philip.

Above: Critics scalded Vancouver's Harry Jerome in 1960, claiming he quit in the Rome Olympics. But two years later Harry was co-holder of the world's record for 100 metres. His detractors quietly disappeared.

Right: Lloyd Percival, called The Coach, was years ahead of his time in all aspects of training and coaching. It was on his book, *The Hockey Manual*, that Soviet team founder Anatoli Tarasov based his theories.

Sandra Post of Oakville, Ontario, was the best golfer Canada ever produced for the U.S. women's tour. At 19, she won the LPGA championship, the top tour event. Later, she won back-to-back Dinah Shore titles.

Right: Jimmy Breslin once wrote that Toronto heavyweight George Chuvalo "fights with his face," but Muhammad Ali needed all his skill to win in 1966.

Below: The Fog Bowl in 1962 was one of the more bizarre Grey Cup games. Mist oozed across Toronto's CNE Stadium and in the fourth quarter was nearly impenetrable. So Commissioner Sydney Halter postponed proceedings for 24 hours. Winnipeg held on to win against Hamilton the next day.

Opposite page: Acrobatic Joe Kapp (22) was nimble enough to avoid tough Tiger-Cat end Pete Neumann and lead B.C. Lions to their first Grey Cup in 1964.

Jersey-clutching seldom stopped rock-ribbed Canadian quarterback Russ Jackson, who helped Ottawa gallop to two Grey Cup triumphs.

Opposite page: Quarterback Ken Ploen hoisted (and heisted) the Grey Cup four times in the six years from 1957 through 1962 when Winnipeg dominated football.

Following page: Beverley Boys, a vivacious blonde from Pickering, Ontario, was queen of the diving boards in the early 1970s. She won Commonwealth Games golds from both the three-metre board and the 10-metre platform.

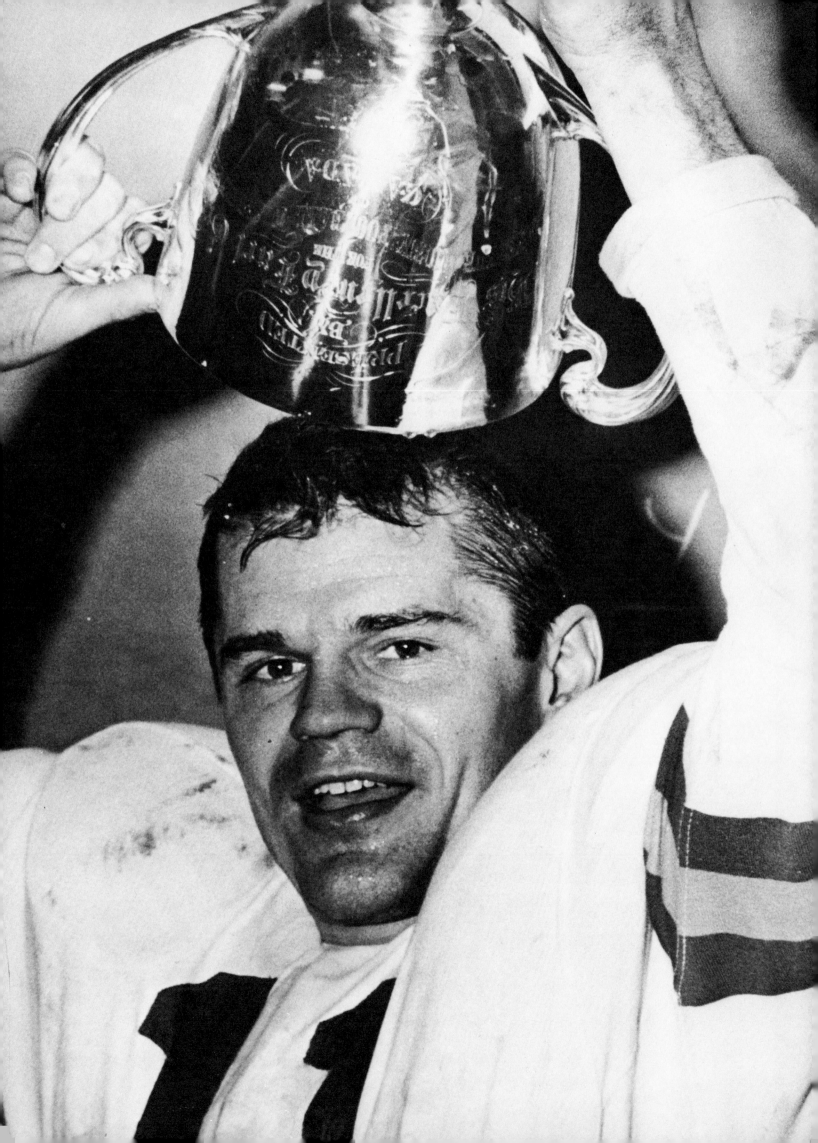

THE 1970s

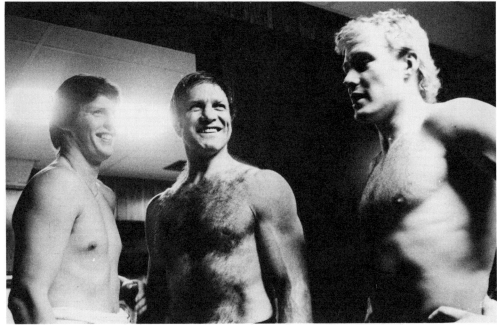

Above: The beginning: Phil Esposito, in the slot, scored the first goal on Vladislav Tretiak as the historic Canada-Soviet series began in 1972.

Left: WHA goaltenders cringed when Winnipeg Jets sent out Ulf Nilsson, Bobby Hull and Anders Hedberg. In 1975, this line scored 177 goals.

The end: Tretiak was down and Paul Henderson up as Canada dramatically won the eight-game series with 34 seconds left.

NUMBER FOUR

In a famous photograph, Bobby Orr is flying through space, a grin on his face, the puck in the net in overtime, and the Boston Bruins are the Stanley Cup champions for the first time in twenty-nine years, escorted there by this clearly identifiable flying object.

Oh, what joy there was then for this star-crossed hero, this prince of defencemen. The year was 1971 and although he had just turned twenty-two, he was completing his fifth year of triumph in the National Hockey League. This goal was the icing on the cake. It capped a season in which Robert Gordon Orr of Parry Sound, Ontario, won the Hart Trophy as the NHL's most valuable player, the James Norris Trophy as the best defenceman, the Conn Smythe Trophy as the outstanding player in the play-offs, the Lou Marsh Trophy as Canada's outstanding athlete, and set records for total assists over a season and for total points by a defenceman.

"The most surprising thing about Orr is that he has anything left to surprise you with," The *Boston Globe*'s grizzled hockey writer Tom Fitzgerald sighed once that season. "You think you've seen the ultimate execution of some beautifully subtle idea. Then he surpasses it. His unplanned moves are the most breathtaking of all. Within his area, this man is a genius."

But Bobby Orr had a relentless antagonist: his spirit. It was at once his greatest asset and an unforgiving foe. At times he soared with it, exploding with the puck in a release of energy and determination and sometimes even jubilation. But every now and then he'd pay an awful price for his intensity. He'd jump toward holes that barely existed between defencemen and the sideboards, and if the defenders closed the gaps in time it was Orr's knees that absorbed the shock.

He wore a Boston uniform during the ten seasons from 1966–67 through 1975–76, but he missed anywhere from two to seventy games in all but three of them. He had five operations on his ravaged left knee (and one on the right knee) including two in that final Boston year that limited his activity to just ten games and persuaded his Bruin bosses to let him sign a contract with the Chicago Black Hawks. And so he did —five years for $3 million—but he played only twenty games that season, none the next, and finally hung up his Number Four forever after six games in the 1978–79 season.

Bobby Orr in full flight was a captivating figure. He was far more spectacular than most of the superstars of the last quarter-century—Gordie Howe, say, or Phil Esposito or Wayne Gretzky, each unmatched on the scoring tables of his time, but largely unprepossessing getting there. Orr was a player of marvellous offensive skills, remarkable puck control, and instant acceleration. He skated on a pair of wide-set slightly bow-legged pins that gave him great balance and a way of shifting direction and speed making him a hard man to keep track of. His acceleration could get him out of his own end before forecheckers could react.

It was equally effective at the other end, too, where, though a left-hand shot, he would park on the right side of the blue line, alert and intense. Indeed, it was on a play from there that he scored the Stanley Cup winner in overtime in 1971. The Bruins and the Blues were locked at 3-3 some forty seconds into extra time, with Boston

Opposite page: Orr popularized offensive play by defencemen, but he was strong defensively, as well. Here he guards Montreal's Henri Richard.

Scoring in overtime, Bobby Orr sent the Stanley Cup to Boston in 1970. Aided by Noel Picard's trip, he flew past the St. Louis net.

Opposite page: Who'd have thought hip L.A. would lend obscurity? It did for great little centre Marcel Dionne, who became nearly invisible with the Kings out there.

pressing. Stationed at the St. Louis line, Orr blocked the puck as it skidded from a mix-up of players near the cage. He zipped it to Derek Sanderson in the corner and burst for the goal, corralled a return pass and flew across the front of the net, potting a backhander as a Blues defender hooked his feet and sent him floating into a bellyflop, yelling in ecstasy as the red light glowed.

Like most hockey players (and unlike almost all baseball players) Orr carried his fame modestly. He took his game seriously, but not himself. He was a star from the start. At fourteen he signed to play for the Oshawa Generals juniors, and for the first year his folks, Doug and Arva Orr, or their neighbours, drove Bobby from Parry Sound, about 140 miles north of Toronto, to the various OHA Junior A cities, and home again afterwards.

There were five Orr kids—Patricia, Ron, Bobby, Penny and Doug, Jr.—growing up in a closely knit family. One night when Oshawa was playing in Hamilton Bobby got in a fight along the boards and wasn't faring too well. Suddenly a woman came leaping across the seats and whacked Orr's opponent over the head with her purse.

"You big brute," cried Pat Orr, "you leave Bobby alone!"

He didn't need anybody to look out for him in the NHL. He was a fiery guy who was rarely an instigator of a fight but not one to back off, either. Rivals tested him early, as they do with rookies, and when they found him willing they let him be. It wasn't Number Four's rivals who did him in; it was his guts.

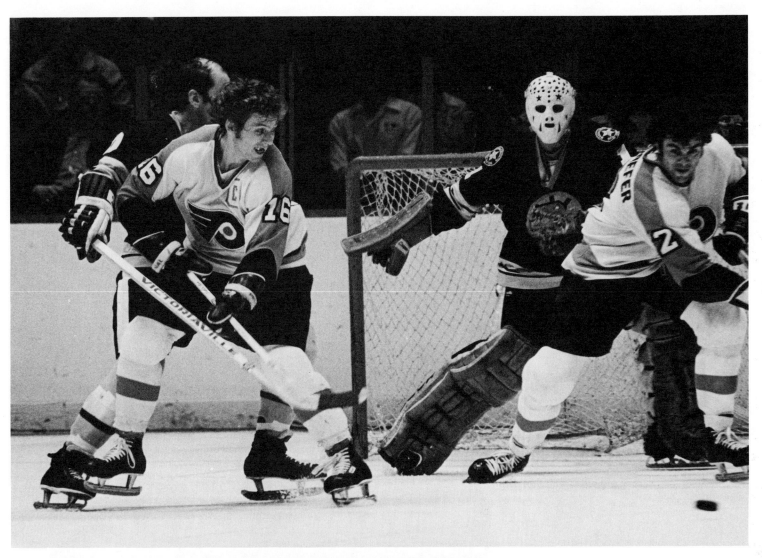

Above and opposite page: Bobby Clarke led Philadelphia to Stanley Cup wins over Boston in 1974 (he and Gary Dornhoefer attack Bruin Eddie Johnston) and Buffalo (Gil Perreault pursues from behind) in a 15-year career.

Left: Darryl Sittler's overtime goal won the 1976 Canada Cup, fooling Czech goaler Vlad Dzurilla. Scout Don Cherry provided the formula: ''Fake a shot. Dzurilla will come out. Shift to your left. He'll have left you plenty of open net.'' Darryl did that, and Don was right on.

Opposite page: When Guy Lafleur was in flight, the Forum legions cried his name. Hair streaming in the wind, he shone for 14 seasons in Montreal.

Gentleman Jean Béliveau played on ten (count 'em, 10) Stanley Cup winners from 1956 through 1971, all with the non-stop Canadiens.

Above: Grey Cup Week lunacy was born in 1948 when Calgary fans disguised themselves as cowpokes on Toronto's Bay Street, and it went on and on. Here, in 1971, a Calgary alderman rides into Vancouver's Georgia Hotel.

Top right: Less than a minute showed on the clock in the 1976 Grey Cup game as Calm Tom Clements (2) outmanoeuvred western pursuit and threw a pass to . . . Tony Gabriel (right) running clear in the Saskatchewan end zone. That was all the Ottawa Rough Riders needed to nail down a 23–20 triumph.

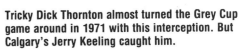

Tricky Dick Thornton almost turned the Grey Cup game around in 1971 with this interception. But Calgary's Jerry Keeling caught him.

Throwing the football, the CFL's all-time all-timer is Ron Lancaster, leader in passes thrown, passes completed and yardage gained.

A great jockey on the greatest thoroughbred, New Brunswick's Ron Turcotte aboard Secretariat. Together they won the Kentucky Derby in record time, the Preakness and, pictured here at New York's Belmont track, the punishing mile and a half Belmont Stakes by 31 lengths.

Canada produces the world's best harness-racing drivers. They learn in rural areas, move to the big Canadian tracks, then become leaders in the U.S. This pattern has been true of (clockwise from left) the late Joe O'Brien, Quebec's Hervé Filion, Ontario's John Campbell and Maritimer Bill O'Donnell.

Above: When the red-and-white clad Canadian team marched into the Olympic Stadium in 1976, the flag-bearer was ex-track star Abbie Hoffman.

Opposite page: The man who made the 1976 Summer Olympics happen, Montreal Mayor Jean Drapeau, addresses the multitude in front of the cross atop Mount Royal.

Following pages: A grey drizzle enfolded a packed Olympic Stadium in 1976 as high-jumping came down to three men. Canada's Greg Joy outdueled U.S. Dwight Stones for the silver medal behind Poland's Jacek Wszola.

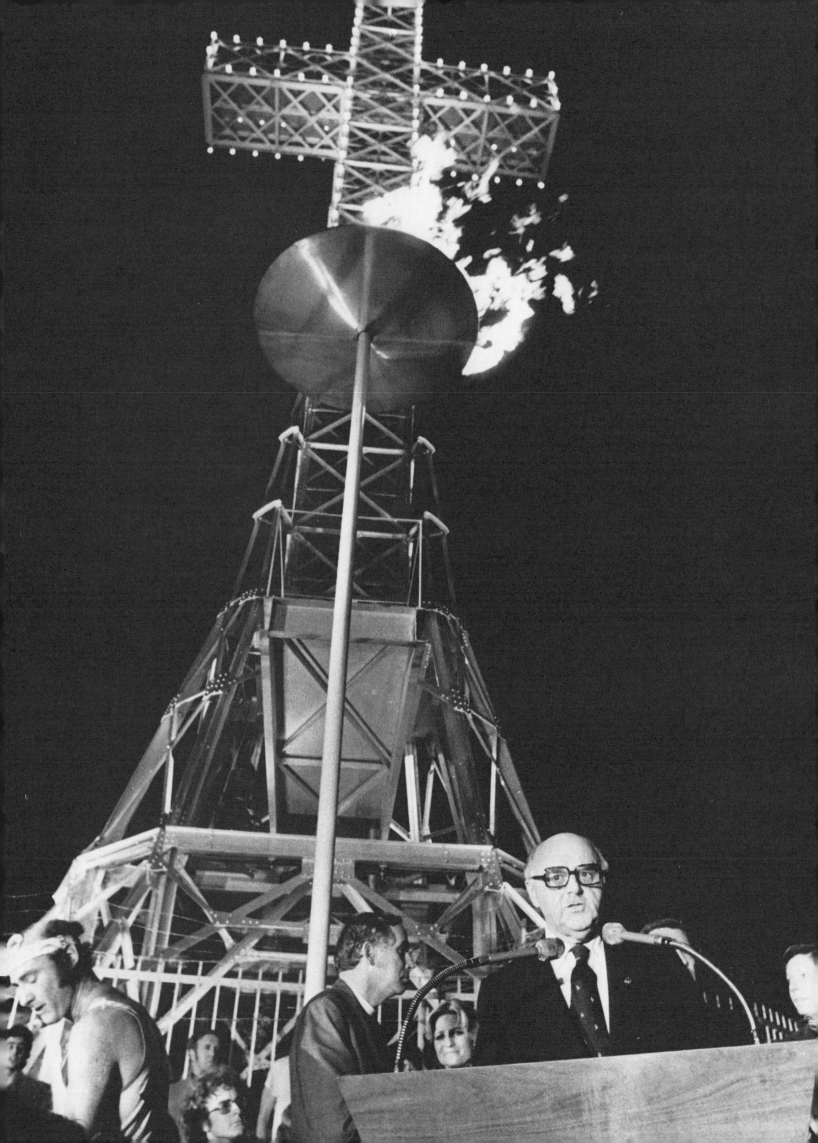

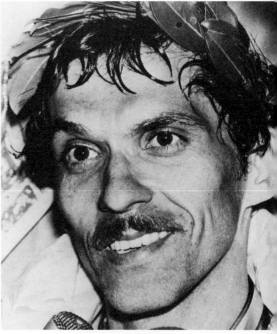

Above: Now everybody's doin' it, doin' it, but in 1970 distance running was a novelty. That's when Jerome Drayton won the Boston Marathon.

Left: Talk about your modern-day Annie Oakleys, here's flowing-haired Susan Nattrass of Edmonton, who knew no peer in trap-shooting.

Opposite page: Edmonton isn't all Oilers and Eskimos. In 1978 Graham Smith tore up the Commonwealth Games pool with six golds. Then the muscled Edmonton individual-medley ace won the 200 metres at the Worlds.

Preceding pages: Cindy Nicholas, now a Toronto lawyer, made a habit of crossing the English Channel without a boat but with awesome strokes in the 1970s.

Above: Slalom star Betsy Clifford chased Nancy Greene as Canada's top performer on European mountain slopes in 1970. The young Ottawa skier scored a stunning win in the giant slalom at Val Gardena in Italy.

Opposite page: The figures of figure skating only bored Toller Cranston, whose skates flashed spectacularly in free-skating routines.

Ken Read was the first Canadian to win a World Cup event when he was first down the hill at Val d'Isère, France, in 1975.

Opposite page: Everyone went wild in Timmins, Ontario, in 1976 when home-town girl Kathy Kreiner, first person down an Innsbruck mountain, won gold. That's Crazy Canuck Jim Hunter holding her up.

Opposite page: Who can forget it? The first man on the moon was Neil Armstrong, the first Blue Jay home run was Doug Ault's. Wow! Then he hit another.

Left: Snow fell as big-league baseball arrived in Toronto on April 7, 1977. So White Sox infielder Jack Brohamer strapped catcher's shin guards to his feet and used bats as ski poles to get into the proper spirit.

Following page: In the early days of the Expos, people stopped breathing (though not permanently) when Le Grand Orange, Rusty Staub, stepped up to the plate.

THE 1980s

THE GREAT ONE

Perhaps there never was a day in hockey's long history more shocking to fans than August 9, 1988, when Wayne Gretzky was traded to the Los Angeles Kings. Because of his stature as virtually a national treasure, Wayne the Wizard had appeared to be as immutable a segment of the Edmonton scene as Jasper Avenue itself. And yet, to the astonishment of millions of fans, the Edmonton owner, Peter Pocklington, sent the game's greatest scorer off to the wilds of Los Angeles. In the words of Paul Coffey, a former teammate and Gretzky's close friend, "You're just a piece of meat."

Though he's gone from Canada, at least once each season there ought to be a mandatory moment of silence for Wayne, a simple bowing of heads before the puck is dropped each autumn. No one in any sport so completely dominated his field in the 1980s, not Jack Nicklaus or Larry Bird or John McEnroe or Martina Navratilova or Reggie Jackson or anybody.

All of us were startled a decade ago that this scrawny blond darting fellow, dominant as Bobby Orr, should come along so soon after Boston's marvellous defenceman was prematurely felled by injured knees. In his rookie season in the NHL, 1979–80, Wayne won the Hart Trophy as the league's most valuable player and the Byng Trophy as the most gentlemanly one. And that was his pattern from then on—magnificent play and a gent. He won the Hart, the most coveted individual award of all, for eight straight seasons, and the scoring championship in his first seven.

And those early years were mere harbingers. He'd first won the Hart as a downy-cheeked boy of nineteen. A couple of years later he stunned eldering fans by scoring ninety-two goals in a 212-point season. The numbers were preposterous, even for the present, helter-skelter, wide-open era. Eons ago, in the time of the immortal Howie Morenz, it was a different game. Morenz was a blur on ice who would wind up behind his net for a rink-length swoop ("He made the 7 on his back look like 777," once groused the great little goaltender, Roy Worters). In 1927–28, Morenz won the NHL scoring championship with thirty-three goals and eighteen assists in the forty-four-game season. And Morenz was miles ahead of everybody that year.

So after Gretzky's 212-point season (it was 1981–82) nothing much Wayne did surprised people. Other players, such as Mike Bossy and Mario Lemieux, would leap into the headlines for this scoring feat or that, but partly they were getting the ink because Wayne had reached a plateau where the extraordinary had become commonplace. What more could be said about him?

For instance, Bossy's laudable feat of scoring fifty goals through nine straight seasons was justifiably acclaimed. Still, by the time Gretzky had played eight NHL seasons his reputation was embellished by so many superlatives that there was scarcely notice of his more than fifty goals in all of them. Unaccustomed injuries took him out of sixteen games in his ninth year (1987–88) and the string was broken.

Who knows when he will wind down? He has said he won't play past thirty, which will take him through the 1990–91 season (he was born January 26, 1961) so he is

Opposite page: **Number 99 is a hard man to halt. He's almost always on the prowl, ever alert for an opposing mistake. When it happens, bang!**

135

young enough to retain his enthusiasm for a few seasons more. A while ago, speaking to the television interviewer Dave Hodge after skidding his five hundreth NHL goal into an empty net, Gretzky said he didn't mind that he'd lifted a gift into the unguarded cage. He'd hit a few posts in his time, too, after fooling goaltenders.

He agreed with Hodge that five hundred represented a tall plateau but he wasn't patting himself on the back, by any means. "Seven or eight hundred is more like it," he said, earnestly enough. "Then you can talk about great."

Only two players have topped seven hundred—Phil Esposito with 710 and Gordie Howe with 801. Yes, Gordie played forever to do it (twenty-six years in the NHL compared to Gretzky's nine) but when Gordie played the game, back-checking was not a meaningless phrase from a foreign tongue.

Constructed nowhere near Howe's rock-boned lines, Gretzky nonetheless has been surprisingly durable. He missed only eight games in his first eight seasons, and tacked on 101 playoff games. So he's been busy. Blinking and grunting, muscled goons have taken runs at him, but he's an elusive waterbug on the ice who somehow performs his magic without challenging the sideboards the way Bobby Orr used to, bursting through narrow holes.

In the springtime in recent years, while most players are restoring their resources, Gretzky and his Edmonton teammates have been prolonging the grind all the way through May, winning four Stanley Cups and dropping a fifth in the final round (to the Islanders), an added drain on the skinny wizard. Sometimes people forget that. A monument, please. Or at least a moment's silence.

Sometimes it's said that Wayne Gretzky floats unscathed through a hockey season but, look, Igor Larianov of the Soviets pins him.

Until he was traded to Pittsburgh, Paul Coffey thrilled Edmonton fans for seven seasons with a fluid skating style and super scoring skills.

Opposite page: Some say the unflappable Grant Fuhr is hockey's best goaltender since Georges Vézina. Often left alone he makes key saves.

When the Islanders had it, this pair had it most:
Denis Potvin (opposite page) and Brian Trottier
(above, checking Gretzky). Ottawa's Potvin led
the defence. Trottier, from Val Marie,
Saskatchewan, provided the offensive thrust.

Right: The Expos' base-stealer supreme all through the 1980s was the versatile Tim Raines, and (opposite page, top) The Hawk, Andre Dawson, was their first real slugger.

Opposite page, bottom: Toronto fans went bananas in August 1984 when Yankee outfielder Dave Winfield threw a ball that hit a bird, rendering same lifeless.

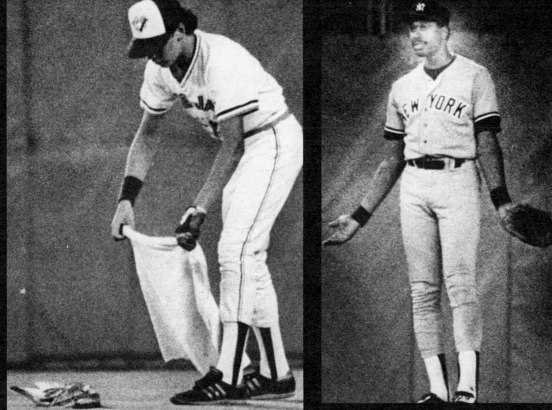

EXPOS AND BLUE JAYS

It was the best of times and the worst of times. It was October 1981 and the valiant Montreal Expos at last had won the championship of the National League East. Or it was October 1985 and the heroic Toronto Blue Jays at last had won the championship of the American League East. What ecstasy! What rewards for the loyal followers! Ah, but what blows were to follow.

Steely-eyed on foreign turf in the playoffs, the Expos and the Blue Jays each climbed to within one victory of a World Series appearance and then, returning home, were done in by men of modest baseball stature, Rick Monday and Jim Sundberg.

For years the patient fans had waited for these towering moments. In Montreal, beginning in 1969 at cosy little Jarry Park, they had sung songs and drunk foamy toasts to Coco Laboy and John Boccabella and Rusty Staub and Boots Day and Bill Lee and a violinist had strolled down the aisle, not once but many times, to dance on the roof of the Expos' third-base dugout, swooping and sweeping, the bow never still.

And in Toronto the fans had fastened upon a sad-sack assortment of heroes in the early, last-place years beginning in 1977—Steve Staggs, Alvis Woods, Jesse Jefferson, Joey McLaughlin, Doug Rader, Mickey Klutts, Dave McKay, Rick Bosetti—all of them, fans and players, joined in the world's worst ballpark, Exhibition Stadium, where the rolling outfield carpet resembled a painting of an ocean's tide and the seats along the first-base side faced centre field instead of the plate.

But finally, in the 1980s, the cellar's woes were swept aside, and first the Expos and then the Blue Jays won division championships and faced Western Division teams for the cherished pennant. The Expos played the Los Angeles Dodgers and the Blue Jays met the Kansas City Royals, and both came home to Canada needing one win in two final games to march into the World Series. In each case, though, the visitors tied the series, forcing a final decisive game.

Fernando Valenzuela, a tubby, wily rookie who peered at the sky as he came through his left-handed motion, pitched for the Dodgers. Ray Burris, a tall, herky-jerky, well-traveled right-hander, was the Expos' choice. Both were in form on the cold grey afternoon of October 19 in cavernous Olympic Stadium, Mayor Jean Drapeau's epic monument to cement.

The Expos scored early. Tim Raines opened with a double, reached third when Valenzuela was late throwing there on Rodney Scott's bunt, and scored as Andre Dawson grounded into a double play.

In the Dodger fifth Rick Monday drove a single, charged to third on Pedro Guerrero's single and jogged in on Valenzuela's roller to second.

The score was unchanged going to the ninth. Burris came out after eight strong innings and Steve Rogers, the Expo ace, who'd won four straight playoff games, retired dangerous Steve Garvey and Ron Cey. He went to 3-and-1 on Monday. Then the Dodger centre-fielder lifted a long fly midway between the 375 and 400-foot signs in right-centre. The ball cleared the wall.

In the Expo ninth, with two out, Gary Carter walked. Larry Parrish walked. The crowd stirred and began a swelling roar. Jerry White stepped in. He had won the third

The Blue Jays have had their high moments as well as their lows. In 1987 George Bell (shown here with Cecil Fielder, left) hit 47 homers and won Most Valuable Player honours.

The tragic moment for the Expos arrived on October 19, 1981. Dodger Rick Monday cost them a World Series berth when he hit a homer off Steve Rogers.

game for the Expos with a three-run homer. The Dodgers brought right-hander Bob Welch from the bullpen. On his first pitch, White grounded to second and the Expos had run out of tomorrows.

The Blue Jays had Doyle Alexander and Dave Stieb ready to pitch the wrap-up games against Kansas City. Doyle had beaten the Yankees a week earlier in the game that clinched the AL East title, but this time the Royals kayoed him. So it was up to Stieb to determine if a World Series was coming to Canada.

A headstrong emotional man, Stieb had pitched two fine games. He won the opener 6-1. He pitched the fourth game, a two-hitter into the seventh inning that became Tom Henke's win when Al Oliver smacked a game-winning double in the ninth.

This time his control did him in, as it had so often before. He trailed 2-1 in the sixth

When the day was done the Expo dugout turned into a tomb. Andre Dawson, Warren Cromartie and Chris Speier sit shaken, hopes shattered.

inning, his team very much in the game. But he walked two men and hit another and now he faced the Kansas City catcher, Jim Sundberg, a veteran the Royals had acquired to stabilize a young pitching staff.

Now, the bases full, Sundberg sliced a fly into a strong wind blowing from left field to right. "It was a fastball, a little inside," reconstructed Sundberg, a right-handed hitter. "I inside-outed it."

The right-fielder, Jesse Barfield, drifted towards the foul-pole, waiting to make the catch. The ball kept angling toward the corner. At the last instant it struck the wire top of the blue-padded fence and bounded back along the carpet. The three runners scored. Sundberg got to third. Suddenly it was 5-1 and the Blue Jays, like the Expos four years before, had run out of tomorrows.

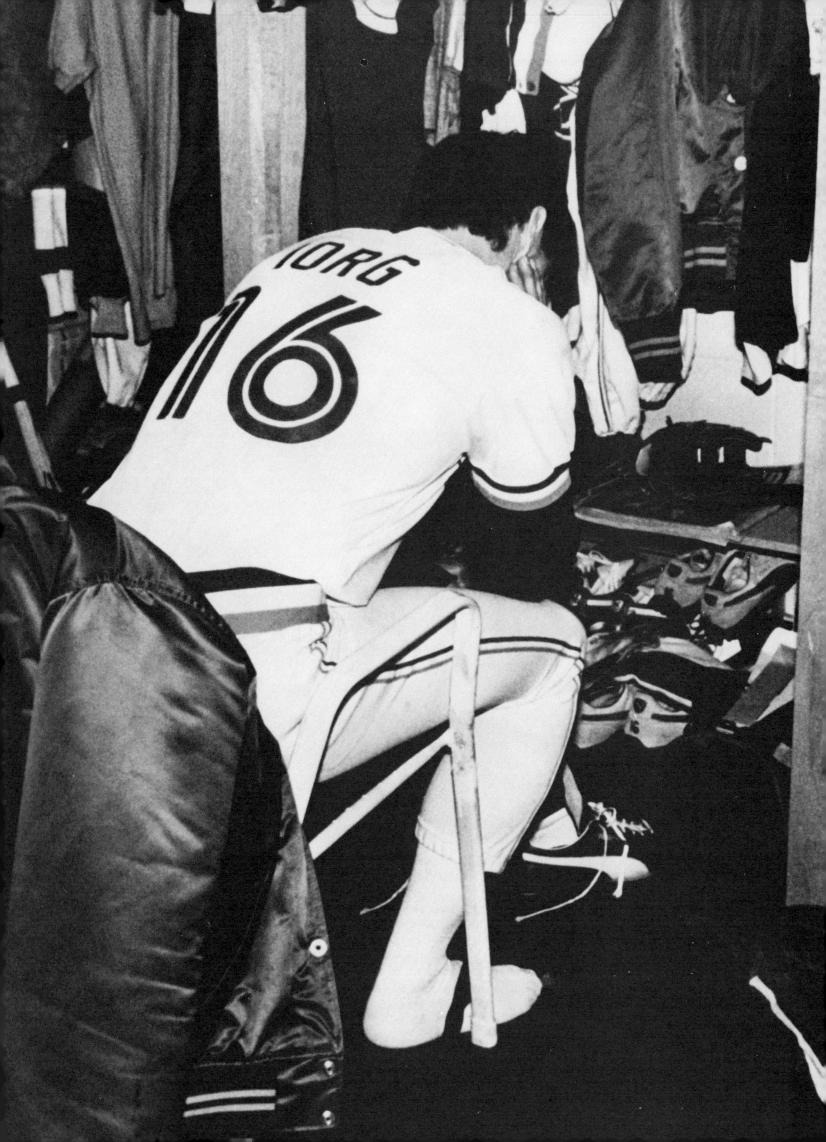

High moments? No, low moments. There was Olympic gold awaiting Canadian fighters Willie DeWit (left) and Shawn O'Sullivan (above) in Los Angeles in 1984, but U.S. heavyweight Henry Tillman handled DeWit and American Frank Tate proved to be too much for welterweight O'Sullivan. The Canadians won silvers.

Opposite page: In 1985, as this picture of infielder Garth Iorg illustrates, the roof fell in on the Blue Jays when Kansas City kept them from the World Series.

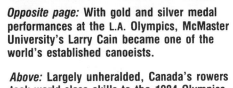

Opposite page: With gold and silver medal performances at the L.A. Olympics, McMaster University's Larry Cain became one of the world's established canoeists.

Above: Largely unheralded, Canada's rowers took world-class skills to the 1984 Olympics, winning six medals. For the first time, the men's eight won gold in a classic stroke-for-stroke duel with the U.S. crew.

Left: Legendary Herman (Jackrabbit) Johanssen spent his 110th birthday in 1985 crediting longevity to canoeing and cross-country skiing.

Above: Montreal's Jacqueline Garneau has her hand raised by Boston Marathon winner Bill Rogers three weeks after the grind. She was second to Rosie Ruiz but then Rosie was disqualified, and Garneau was named the women's winner.

Left: Close but no cigar. Canadian cyclist Steve Bauer was nipped by U.S. cyclist Alexi Grewall in 1984's Olympic individual road race. He won a silver medal.

Opposite page: Nobody was better on a bike than Toronto's Jocelyn Lovell until 1983 when a traffic accident left him paralyzed. In the 1970s Jocelyn won gold medals at both the Commonwealth and the Pan-Am Games.

Warm and modest, Gaetan Boucher was the talk
of the 1984 Winter Olympics, champion at 1,000
and 1,500 metres, bronze medalist at 500.

Kings of the Hill—here are the Crazy Canucks
at Val d'Isère in December, 1980: Dave Murray,
Ken Read, Steve Podborski, Dave Irwin, Chris
Kent and Robin McLeish. Five of them placed
in the top ten finishers for Canada's best men's
World Cup result ever.

Ebullient Marilyn Darte peers past a Swedish curler at the women's 1986 championship bonspiel. Darte and her vice-skip Kathy McEdwards (standing) helped bring the title home to Canada.

The Brier is the biggest curling event in Canada
year after year, and one of the top skips is
Ontario's Ed Werenich, here taking aim.

Snooker is a big television attraction in Britain, so in 1987 Canada's kingpin with a cue, Cliff Thorburn, moved there and became a champion.

Race officials examine the remains of a
Formula I Ferrari driven by Canadian Gilles
Villeneuve in Belgium. The great Quebec driver
(left) was killed.

Two quarterbacks who ignited Canadian crowds before defecting to the U.S. pros could run and throw that football. Dieter Brock (opposite page) threw sidearm zingers for Winnipeg and Warren Moon (above) was a galloping Eskimo.

Right: Hugh Campbell practically owns the Grey Cup. He spent six years coaching the Edmonton Eskimos and made six Cup appearances, winning five. In his two years as general manager, his Esks have been there twice, and are 1-1.

No one gave underdog Ottawa a chance against the bruising Eskimos in 1981's Grey Cup game. But it took this last-minute field goal by Dave Cutler to put down the Rough Riders, 26–23.

Opposite page: Until he retired in 1988, Alex Baumann, who had a maple leaf tattooed over his heart, was the world's premier individual-medley swimmer—freestyle, back, breast and butterfly. He held world records at 200 and 400 metres.

Carling Bassett got to Wimbledon's fourth round in 1986. She later married U.S. tennis tourist Bob Seguso and became a mom.

Opposite page: Tempestuous Victor Davis set records and startled a queen with equal vigour. Elizabeth II blinked in surprise when he kicked a water bucket in Brisbane. At the L.A. Games he set a world record, winning the 200 metres breast stroke.

Few countries have produced athletes as
courageous as Terry Fox (heading down the
road in a typical heart-rending scene) and Steve
Fonyo (right).

Above: Twice in four days Banff's Karen Percy swept down Mount Allan at Calgary's Winter Olympics to win bronze medals in alpine skiing.

Right: Ice-dancing stars in Calgary's spectacular Games were Tracy Wilson and Rob McCall, fluid performers who earned a bronze medal in a strong field.

Opposite page: There was only praise for Calgary's presentation of the 1988 Winter Olympics and only joy on the faces of Canada's opening-day contingent marching into McMahon Stadium behind flag-bearer Brian Orser.

THE FASTEST HUMAN

I t took a while for Ben Johnson's adopted homeland to grow excited about the world's fastest human. Partly this was because Canadians take a long time to accept other Canadians as being much good at anything, and partly it's because Ben is a man who lets his feet do the talking.

But eventually, with the sports world set agog by Ben's record 100-metre trip in Rome in 1987, his fellow citizens began accepting Ben as a sort of sprinting Wayne Gretzky (could anything be finer?).

Ben's self-effacement in a world dizzy with hype is monumental and perhaps unique. On the soft August evening in Rome when he ran faster than anyone had ever run— 100 metres in 9.83 seconds—he scarcely cracked a smile when he glanced at the electronic scoreboard. He jogged part way around the track amid the pandemonium of 64,500 spectators, his face solemn, his round eyes large. He had no words for Charlie Francis, his coach. He just shook his hand, nodding once.

Ben and Charlie first got together late in 1976. Ben was a stripling of ninety-three pounds, just turned fifteen, coming north with his mother and two sisters from Jamaica. His older brother, Edward, a minister, took young Ben to a Toronto track where Charlie Francis trained sprinters.

Ben never shows excitement, never has, may never. The contrast between him and his foremost rival, the American Carl Lewis, is quite stunning. Lewis is coiffured and hip and even elegant, and prior to the 1984 Olympics he was built into a cosmic figure. Perhaps you'll recall how *Time* magazine strove valiantly for restraint in describing him:

"What he does is so simple, and how he does it so complicated, that Carl Lewis is a basic mystery. How fast he runs, how far he jumps, may serve to establish the precise lengths to which men can go. Gentler than a superman, more delicate than the common perception of a strongman, Lewis is physically the most advanced human being in the world, and about to become the most famous global sports figure since Muhammad Ali."

This reserved account was okay with Carl. "There are going to be some absolutely unheard of things coming from me," Carl said. And of the Olympics he added, "I am here to make money." Baron Pierre de Coubertin of France, the founder of the modern Olympic movement, could not have said it better.

This is what Ben was up against during the three years following the Los Angeles Olympics. He began beating Lewis regularly in 1986, but Carl said he was unconcerned because 1986 was an off-year for him. He was gearing for the 1987 world championships in Rome.

Meantime, quiet Ben just kept winning. At the Commonwealth Games in July in Edinburgh, it became apparent that there's something anticlimactic about watching a world champion streak 100 metres. Almost the moment he starts, he's finished. In baseball terms, it's like running from the plate to first base in 2.7 seconds.

You see Ben and his rivals stir restlessly near their starting blocks in the minutes

Opposite page: Here is the sensational moment when Ben Johnson's finishing kick told American Carl Lewis that his hot pursuit would fail.

Following pages: A film reprint from the official timer camera shows Ben's clear margin over Lewis in 9.83 seconds, making him world's fastest human.

before they explode out of them. Clad in warm-up suits they bounce on the rust-coloured, pebbled track, once, twice, half a dozen times. Or they pace a few strides down the track, break into little jogs, knees kicking high, then slowly retrace their steps, heads bent in concentration. A whistle cuts the air and the crowd is completely still as the warm-up suits come off and the sprinters step gingerly into the metal starting blocks, crouch briefly on one knee, then nervously adjust their spiked feet in the blocks, and place their fingers along the white starting line.

In Rome, Ben and Lewis are crouched in adjoining lanes. Their fingertips are only eight inches apart as they back into the blocks, but not a look or a word is exchanged. In the press box the *Globe and Mail*'s James Christie glues field glasses on them. Ben's eyes are straight ahead, the whites contrasting sharply with his ebony complexion. Lewis stares fixedly at the track beneath him.

"Set!" cries the starter.

They're up, hunched.

The gun cracks.

Ben comes from the blocks with exquisite timing, wide-legged, arms cutting the air, teeth clenched. "He looks like a ferocious fullback," Christie cries.

The field moves in a bunch, a human bouquet, faces taut, every muscle fighting to get out of the restraining skin. There's a moment to observe Ben's hugely-muscled shoulders and biceps, the arms swinging low past his hips as he pumps them, the dark legs hammering in short, cruel strides.

Suddenly they're all past the finish line, pulling up in long jarring strides, chests heaving, and Ben Johnson has done it again, beaten the fast-closing Lewis, who finishes in his best time ever, 9.93, but not fast enough to overtake this man in front, the world's fastest human.

INDEX TO PHOTOGRAPHS

PHOTOGRAPH CREDITS

Claus Andersen, 17
Athlete Information Bureau, 5, 152, 154
Bruce Bennett/NHL Publishing, 19, 21 bottom
Ottmar Bierwagen, 32, 169 right
Denis Brodeur, 21 top, 22
Canada's Sports Hall of Fame, 46, 60, 66, 68, 70, 84 top, 86 top, 86 bottom, 92 bottom, 94 top, 100, 123 right, 123 left, 159
Canada Wide Feature Service, 1, 24–25, 26, 27, 29, 30, 50, 63 left, 64, 67, 69, 73 bottom right, 84 bottom left, 84 bottom right, 87, 88, 90, 94 bottom, 98, 99, 117 bottom, 117 top left, 117 top centre, 117 top right, 122, 130, 131, 138
Canadian Football Hall of Fame, 72, 73 bottom left
Canapress, 8, 12, 14, 28, 42, 47, 52, 53, 54, 63 right, 65, 66 bottom left, 66 right, 73 top, 76, 85, 91, 93, 96 top, 96 bottom, 97, 102 top, 106, 112 top left, 112 top right, 112 bottom, 113, 114–115, 116 top, 118, 119, 120–121, 124–125, 126, 127, 132, 141, 142, 143 top, 143 bottom, 144, 146, 147, 148, 149 top,

149 bottom, 150, 151 top, 151 bottom, 153 left, 153 right, 156, 157, 159 top, 160 bottom, 161, 162, 164, 165, 167, 170, 172–173
Angelo Cavalli/Ski Canada Magazine, 31
The Globe and Mail, 163
Hockey Hall of Fame, 40, 44–45, 83
Serge Lang, 155
Deanne Conacher Leuty, 11
Doug McLellan/NHL Publishing, 16, 20
Jean-Paul Maeder, 128
Bob Mummery/NHL Publishing, 134
NHL Publishing, 2–3, 23, 34, 56, 58, 59, 82 top, 82 bottom, 102 bottom, 104, 107, 109 top, 109 bottom, 110, 111, 137, 139, 140
Ontario Archives, 36, 80 bottom
Robert Orr, 18
Public Archives of Canada, 41, 48, 57, 78–79, 80 top, 81, 92 top, 108, 129
Ian Tomlinson, 169 left
City of Toronto Archives, 37, 38
Toronto Star Syndicate, 103, 158, 160 top, 166
Nick Volpe, 74–75
Jim Wiley, 168